HAL•LEONARD®
DRUM PLAY-ALONG™

AUDIO ACCESS INCLUDED

VOL. 27

MODERN WORSHIP

T0081987

PLAYBACK+
Speed • Pitch • Balance • Loop

To access audio visit:
www.halleonard.com/mylibrary

Enter Code
8907-6164-2921-5971

ISBN 978-1-61780-433-5

HAL•LEONARD®

Visit Hal Leonard Online at
www.halleonard.com

Contact Us:
Hal Leonard
7777 West Bluemound Road
Milwaukee, WI 53213
Email: info@halleonard.com

In Europe contact:
Hal Leonard Europe Limited
42 Wigmore Street
Marylebone, London, W1U 2RN
Email: info@halleonardeurope.com

In Australia contact:
Hal Leonard Australia Pty. Ltd.
4 Lentara Court
Cheltenham, Victoria, 3192 Australia
Email: info@halleonard.com.au

CONTENTS

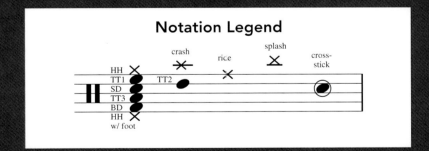

Beautiful One

Words and Music by Tim Hughes

Days of Elijah

Words and Music by Robin Mark

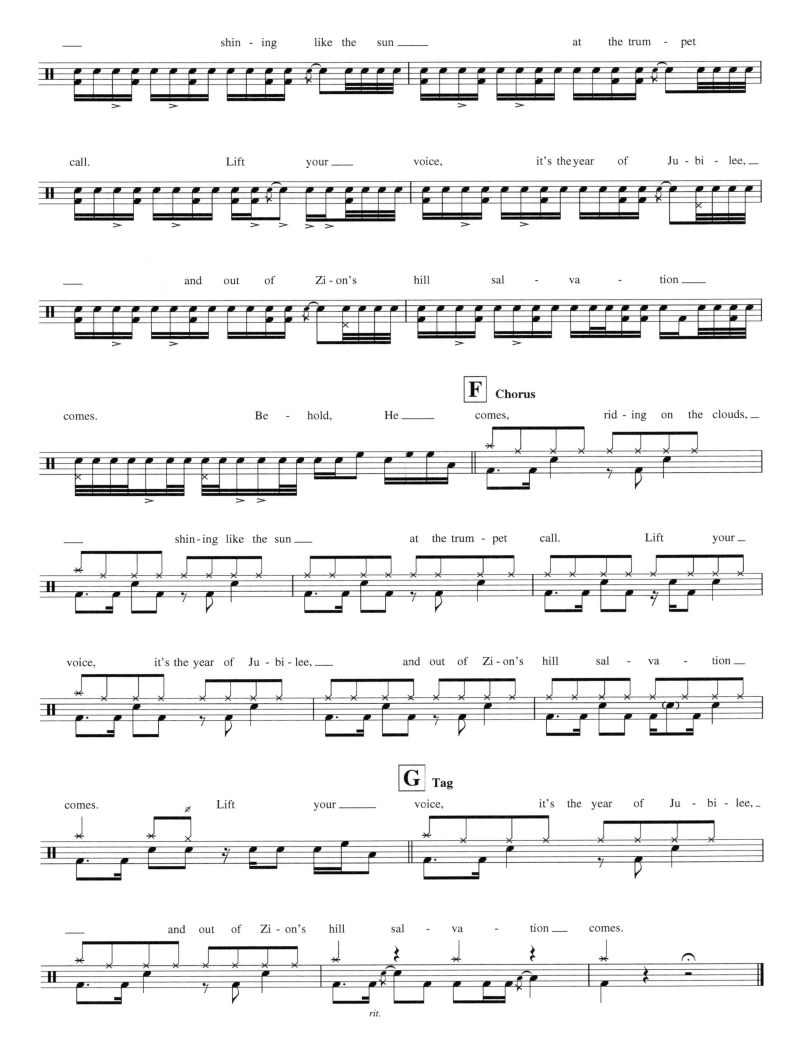

Hear Our Praises

Words and Music by Reuben Morgan

Holy Is the Lord

Words and Music by Chris Tomlin and Louie Giglio

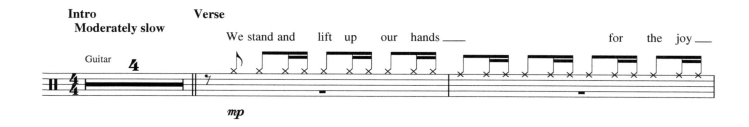

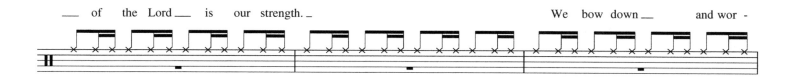

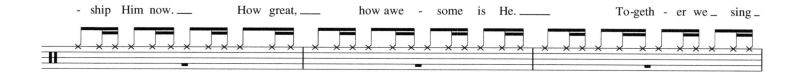

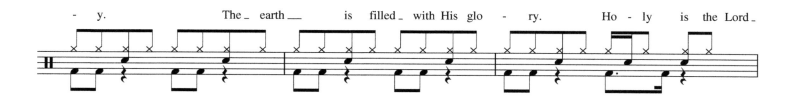

Bridge

Chorus

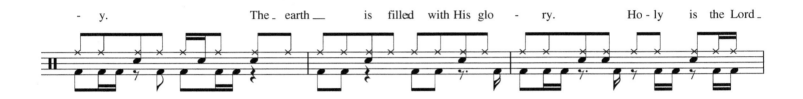

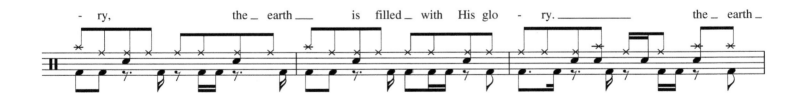

How Great Is Our God

Words and Music by Chris Tomlin, Jesse Reeves and Ed Cash

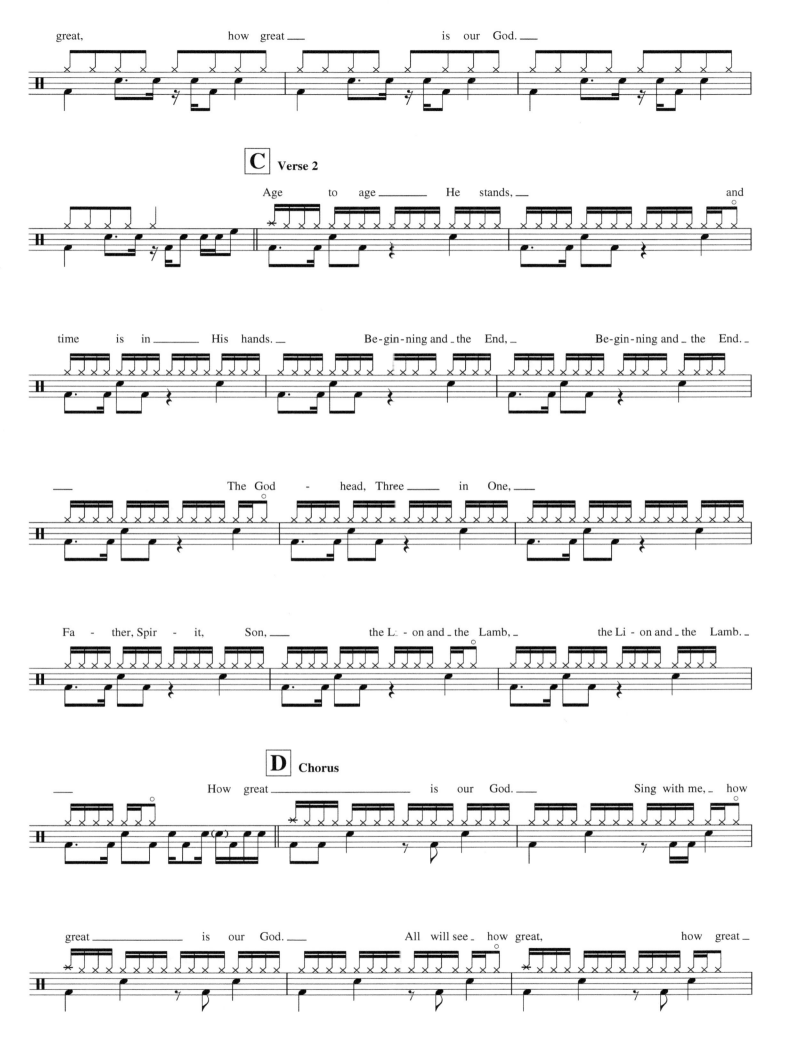

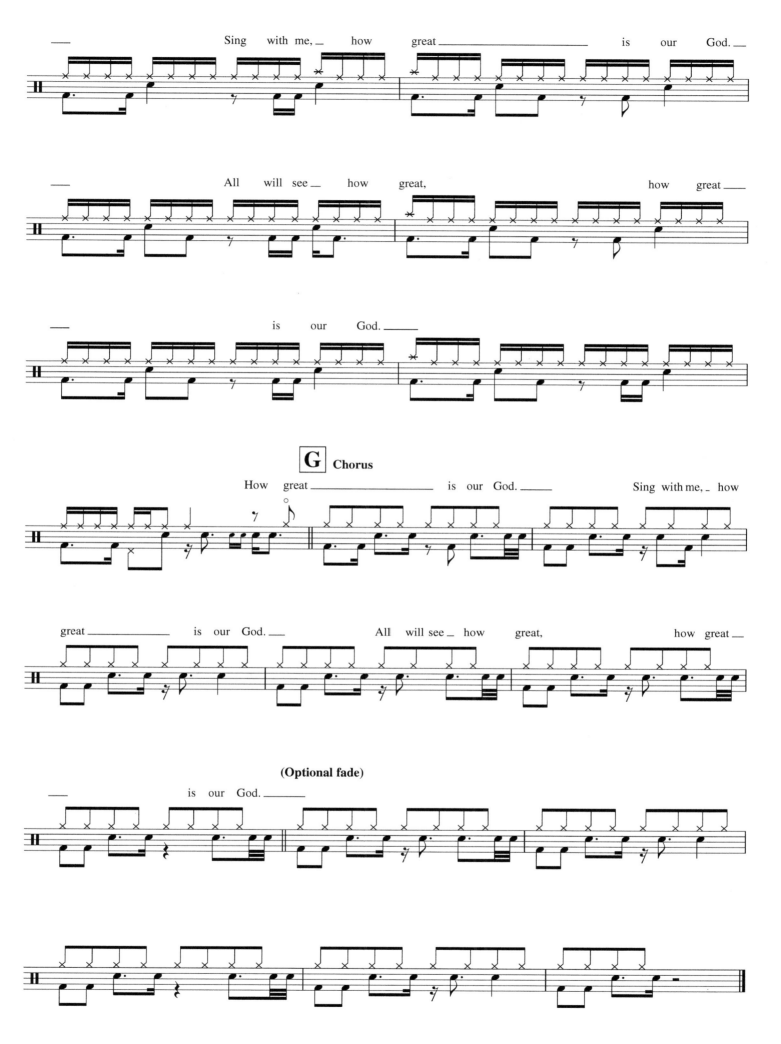

I Give You My Heart

Words and Music by Reuben Morgan

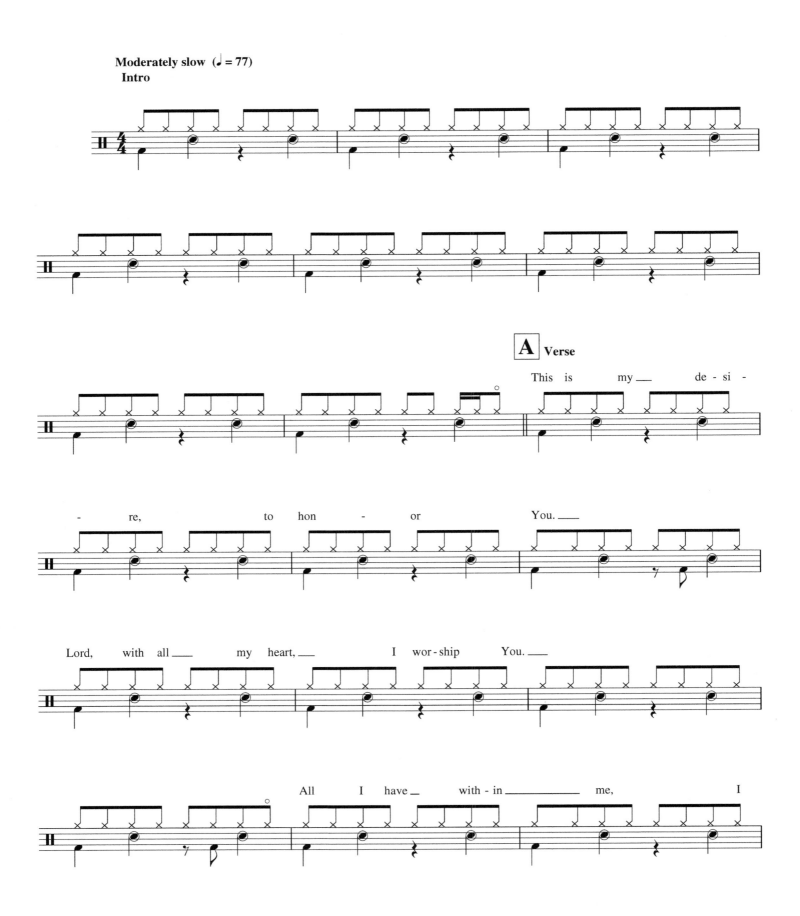

D Chorus

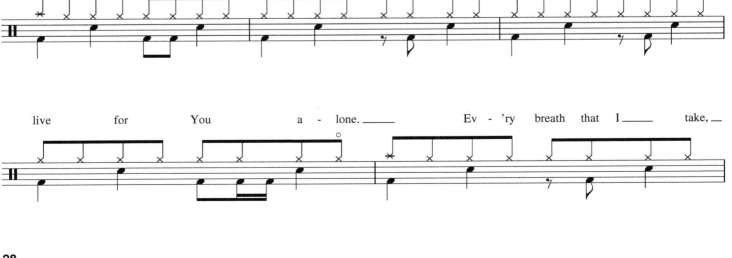

Worthy Is the Lamb

Words and Music by Darlene Zschech

You Are Holy
(Prince of Peace)

Words and Music by Marc Imboden and Tammi Rhoton

BEAUTIFUL ONE

TIM HUGHES

Key of **D Major**, 4/4

INTRO:

G   A   Bm7   A

G   A   D

VERSE 1:

G   A   D/F♯
Wonderful, so wonderful is Your unfailing love

  G   A   Bm7
Your cross has spoken mercy over me

  G   A   D/F♯
No eye has seen, no ear has heard, no heart could fully know

  G   A   D
How glorious, how beautiful You are

CHORUS:

    G A   G A
Beautiful One I love, Beautiful One I adore

    G A   D
Beautiful One, my soul must sing

VERSE 2:

G   A   D/F♯
Powerful, so powerful, Your glory fills the skies

  G   A   Bm7
Your mighty works displayed for all to see

  G   A   D/F♯
The beauty of Your majesty awakes my heart to sing:

  G   A   D
How marvelous, how wonderful You are

(REPEAT CHORUS 2X)

BRIDGE (2X):

  G   A
You opened my eyes to Your wonders anew

  G   A
You captured my heart with this love

   G   A   D
'Cause nothing on earth is as beautiful as You

(REPEAT CHORUS 2X)

DAYS OF ELIJAH

ROBIN MARK

Key of **G Major, 4/4**

INTRO (2X):

G   C   G   D

VERSE 1:

G   C   G   D   G
These are the days of Elijah, declaring the word of the Lord

   G   C   G   D   G
And these are the days of Your servant Moses, righteousness being restored

    Bm   Em   Am   C   Dsus   D
And though these are days of great trials, of famine and darkness and sword

   G   C   G   D   G
Still we are the voice in the desert crying, "Prepare ye the way of the Lord!"

CHORUS:

  D   G   C
Behold, He comes, riding on the clouds

          G   D
Shining like the sun at the trumpet call

       G   C
Lift your voice, it's the year of Jubilee

          G   D   G   (C   G   D)
And out of Zion's hill salvation comes

VERSE 2:

   G   C   G   D   G
And these are the days of Ezekiel, the dry bones becoming as flesh

   G   C   G   D   G
And these are the days of Your servant David, rebuilding a temple of praise

    Bm   Em   Am   C   Dsus   D
And these are the days of the harvest, the fields are as white in Your world

   G   C   G   D   G
And we are the laborers in Your vineyard, declaring the word of the Lord

(REPEAT CHORUS 3X)

TAG:

D   G   C
Lift your voice, it's the year of Jubilee

          G   D   G (hold)
And out of Zion's hill salvation comes

HEAR OUR PRAISES

REUBEN MORGAN

Key of **C Major**, 4/4

INTRO:

C   Csus   C   Csus

VERSE 1:

C   Csus   C   G/B
    May our homes be filled with dancing
Am   F   Gsus   G
    May our streets be filled with joy
C   Csus   C   G/B
    May injustice bow to Jesus
Am   F   Gsus   G
    As the people turn to pray

CHORUS:

        C   G/B   F/A
From the mountain   to the valley

        Am   Em7   F   Gsus
Hear our praises   rise to You

        C   G/B   F/A
From the heavens   to the nations

        Am   Em7   F   Gsus
Hear the singing   fill the air

(REPEAT INTRO)

VERSE 2:

C   Csus   C   G/B
    May our light shine in the darkness
Am   F   Gsus   G
    As we walk before the cross
C   Csus   C   G/B
    May Your glory fill the whole earth
Am   F   Gsus   G
    As the water o'er the seas

(REPEAT CHORUS)

TRANSITION TO BRIDGE:

C (2 bars)

BRIDGE (2X):

   F   Dm7   Am   Em7
Hallelujah,   hallelujah
   F   Dm7   Gsus   G
Hallelujah,   hallelujah

(REPEAT CHORUS 2X)

OUTRO:

C   Csus   C   Csus   C (hold)

HOLY IS THE LORD

CHRIS TOMLIN and LOUIE GIGLIO

Key of **G Major**, 4/4

INTRO (GUITAR ONLY):

G Csus2 D

G Csus2 D

VERSE:

G   Csus2   D
We stand and lift up our hands

     G/B   Csus2   D
For the joy of the Lord is our strength

G   Csus2   D
We bow down and worship Him now

G/B   Csus2   D
How great, how awesome is He

      A7sus   Csus2
Together we sing

CHORUS:

     G/B Csus2 Dsus D
Holy is the Lord God Almighty

  Em7 Csus2   Dsus
The earth is filled with His glory

D   G/B Csus2 Dsus D
Holy is the Lord God Almighty

  Em7 Csus2   Dsus D
The earth is filled with His glory

  Em7 Csus2   Dsus D
The earth is filled with His glory

(REPEAT VERSE & CHORUS)

BRIDGE:

  G   D/F♯
It's rising up all around

     F   C
It's the anthem of the Lord's renown

  G   D/F♯
It's rising up all around

     F   C
It's the anthem of the Lord's renown

       A7sus Cadd2
And together we sing

     A7sus Cadd2
Everyone sing

(REPEAT CHORUS)

(REPEAT LAST LINE OF CHORUS)

END ON G

HOW GREAT IS OUR GOD

CHRIS TOMLIN, JESSE REEVES and ED CASH

Key of **G Major, 4/4**

INTRO:

G (2 bars)

VERSE 1:

    G   **Em7**
The splendor of the King, clothed in majesty

            Cmaj7
Let all the earth rejoice, all the earth rejoice

    G   **Em7**
He wraps Himself in light, and darkness tries to hide

            Cmaj7
It trembles at His voice, trembles at His voice

CHORUS:

    G
How great is our God. Sing with me

   Em7
How great is our God. All will see

  Cmaj7   **D**   **G**
How great, how great is our God

VERSE 2:

G   **Em7**
Age to age He stands, and time is in His hands

       Cmaj7
Beginning and the End, Beginning and the End

    G   **Em7**
The God-head, Three in One, Father, Spirit, Son

      Cmaj7
The Lion and the Lamb, the Lion and the Lamb

(REPEAT CHORUS)

BRIDGE:

G   **Em7**
Name above all names, worthy of all praise

  Cmaj7   **D**   **G**
My heart will sing: How great is our God!

     G   **Em7**
He's the Name above all names, worthy of all praise

  Cmaj7   **D**   **G**
My heart will sing: How great is our God!

(REPEAT CHORUS 2X)

I GIVE YOU MY HEART

REUBEN MORGAN

Key of **D Major, 4/4**

INTRO:

Gmaj7   A/G   F♯m7   Bm7
Gmaj7   A/G   F♯m7   G/A

VERSE:

D   A/C♯ Bm7
This is my de - sire

   G   D   A
To hon - or You

Bm7   A/C♯   D
Lord, with all   my   heart

       Cmaj7   G   A
I worship You

D   A/C♯   Bm7
All I have with - in me

  G   D   A
I give You praise

Bm7   A/C♯   D
All that I a - dore

    Cmaj7   G   A
Is in You

CHORUS:

D   A
Lord, I give You my heart

        Em7
I give You my soul

 G/A
I live for You alone

D   A/C♯
Ev'ry breath that I take

        Em7
Ev'ry moment I'm awake

  G/A   **(Gmaj7 A/G G/A)**
Lord, have Your way in me

(REPEAT VERSE)

(REPEAT CHORUS 2X)

OUTRO:

Gmaj7   A/G   F♯m7   Bm7
Gmaj7   A/G   F♯m7   G/A   D (hold)

WORTHY IS THE LAMB

DARLENE ZSCHECH

Key of **G Major, 4/4**

INTRO:

Em7   G   Em7   G

VERSE:

      C   **G/B**
Thank You for the cross, Lord

      C **D** **G**
Thank You for the price You paid

      D/E **Em7** **D** **C**
Bearing all my sin and shame, in love You came

  Am7 **G/B** **D**
And gave amazing grace

G   **G/B** **C**   **G/B**
Thank You for this love, Lord

     C **D**   **G**
Thank You for the nail-pierced hands

     D/E **Em7** **D** **C**
Washed me in Your cleansing flow, now all I know:

  Am7 **G/B** **D**
Your forgiveness and embrace

CHORUS:

G   **D/F♯** **Am7** **G/B** **C**
Worthy is the Lamb, seated on the throne

D   **D/C** **G/B** **C**   **Am7** **C/G** **D** **D/F♯**
Crown You now with many crowns, You reign victorious

G   **D/F♯** **Am7** **G/B** **C**
High and lifted up, Jesus, Son of God

  D   **D/C** **G/B** **C** **Dsus**
The Treasure of heaven crucified

   Am7 **G/B** **C**
Worthy is the Lamb

   Am7 **G/B** **Dsus**
Worthy is the Lamb

(REPEAT VERSE)

(REPEAT CHORUS 2X)

TAG:

      Am7 **G/B** **C**
Worthy is the Lamb

      Am7 **G/B** **Dsus**
Worthy is the Lamb

       G (hold)
Worthy is the Lamb

YOU ARE HOLY (PRINCE OF PEACE)

MARC IMBODEN and TAMMI RHOTON

Key of **G Major**, 4/4

INTRO (EIGHT BARS):

G   G/C   **Dsus D Dsus2 D**

G   G/C   **Dsus D Dsus2 D**

VERSE:

G(add2)   *Echo:*
You are holy   *(You are holy)*

C(add2)
You are mighty   *(You are mighty)*

Am7
You are worthy   *(You are worthy)*

D
Worthy of praise *(worthy of praise)*

G(add2)
I will follow   *(I will follow)*

C(add2)2
I will listen   *(I will listen)*

Am7
I will love You   *(I will love You)*

D   **G**   **D**   **G**
All of my days *(all of my days)*

CHORUS
(Part I and Part II sung simultaneously):

PART I

Csus2   **Dsus**
I will sing to and worship

Em7   **G/B**
The King who is worthy

Csus2   **Dsus**
And I will love and adore Him

Em7   **G/B**
And I will bow down before Him

Csus2   **Dsus**
And I will sing to and worship

Em7   **G/B**
The King who is worthy

Csus2   **Dsus**
And I will love and adore Him

Em7   **Asus**   **A**
And I will bow down before Him

C(add2)
You're my Prince of Peace

D   **G**
And I will live my life for You.

(REPEAT VERSE)

(REPEAT CHORUS 2X)

TAG:

Csus2
You're my Prince of Peace

D   **G**
And I will live my life for You

PART II

Csus2   **Dsus**
You are Lord of lords, You are King of kings

Em7   **G/B**
You are mighty God, Lord of everything

Csus2   **D**
You're Emmanuel, You're the Great I AM

Em7   **G/B**
You're the Prince of Peace, who is the Lamb

Csus2   **Dsus**
You're the Living God, You're my saving grace

Em7   **G/B**
You will reign forever, You are Ancient of Days

Csus2   **Dsus**
You are Alpha, Omega, Beginning and End

Em7   **Asus**   **A**
You're my Savior, Messiah, Redeemer and Friend

C(add2)
You're my Prince of Peace

D   **G**
And I will live my life for You

HAL·LEONARD® DRUM PLAY-ALONG

AUDIO ACCESS INCLUDED

The Drum Play-Along™ Series will help you play your favorite songs quickly and easily! Just follow the drum notation, listen to the audio to hear how the drums should sound, and then play-along using the separate backing tracks. The lyrics are also included for reference. The audio files are enhanced so you can adjust the recording to any tempo without changing pitch!

HAL·LEONARD®

Visit Hal Leonard Online at
www.halleonard.com

Prices, contents and availability subject to change without notice and may vary outside the US.